MICHAE[

GW01035619

First published in 2008 by
Liberties Press
Guinness Enterprise Centre | Taylor's Lane | Dublin 8 | Ireland
www.LibertiesPress.com
General and sales enquiries: +353 (1) 415 1224 | peter@libertiespress.com
Editorial: +353 (1) 415 1287 | sean@libertiespress.com

Trade enquiries to CMD Distribution
55A Spruce Avenue | Stillorgan Industrial Park | Blackrock | County
Dublin
Tel: +353 (1) 294 2560 | Fax: +353 (1) 294 2564

Distributed in the United States by
Dufour Editions
PO Box 7 | Chester Springs | Pennsylvania | 19425

and in Australia by
James Bennett Pty Limited | InBooks
3 Narabang Way | Belrose NSW 2085

Copyright © Michael Dwyer, 2008

The author has asserted his moral rights.

ISBN: 978–1–905483–50-1

2 4 6 8 10 9 7 5 3 1

A CIP record for this title is available from the British Library.

Design Ros Murphy
Printed in Ireland By Colour Books

MICHAEL DWYER'S

FILM
QUIZ
BOOK

IRISH, HOLLYWOOD AND WORLD CINEMA

In memory of the late Sean Mason, a great friend with a deep appreciation of cinema and a trove of movie knowledge which he passed on to me in Tralee

Contents

Contents

Contents

Contents

Contents

Introduction

I discovered the pleasures of movies when I was very young and living in my home town of Tralee, which had three cinemas at the time. My parents, Nicholas and Mary, were avid cinemagoers, and from when I was four years old, they took me with them to the 7PM shows two or three nights a week. I was further fuelling my addiction on weekends, taking in double-bill matinées on Saturdays and Sundays with my school friends.

I realised just how hooked I was on movies through the deep sense of deprivation I felt over my last three years of secondary school as a boarder at St Brendan's College in Killarney. There we were shown just a single movie each month – chosen randomly, it seemed, by our projectionist priest from a catalogue.

It never occurred to me back then that I might make a living from writing about movies. In my teens, I kept copious notes on all the many films I saw, but they were for my eyes only. Through a fortuitous series of circumstances – my immersion in Tralee Film Society and my subsequent job with the Dublin-based umbrella organisation for Irish film clubs – I was invited to review movies on pirate radio station Big D by Ken Finlay, and then for *In Dublin* magazine, a vibrant, exciting place to work in those days, when John S. Doyle was editor and Colm Toibín was features editor.

Introduction

One of the staples in the Christmas edition of that magazine became the annual film quiz; I derived sadistic pleasure from compiling it. The quiz generated a highly enthusiastic response, which encouraged me to devise a film quiz every Christmas after I moved to the *Sunday Tribune* and then to the *Irish Times* – until the mass of movie information on the Internet made things all too easy.

I recommend that you stay off-line as you work through the five hundred questions in this book. Some are easy, some are fairly difficult, and some are quite devious. And some of the answers are not easily available online.

The book is designed to be enjoyed on a solitary basis, or among friends testing each other's film knowledge. Almost all of the fifty rounds are themed, and each is named after a movie title. If you really want to test yourself, try to name the directors, stars and release dates of the movies named at the head of each round. Be warned: some are very obscure indeed. The answers are available at *www.libertiespress.com*.

Most of all, I trust that the book will make an entertaining read, and that, even if you don't know many of the answers, the information contained in the answers will be interesting or amusing.

Introduction

My thanks to Seán O'Keeffe and Peter O'Connell at Liberties Press for all their encouragement with this project; to Patrick Redmond for the cover picture; to Brian Jennings, for his patience and good humour as the sounding board on any number of quiz questions retained or abandoned; and to Martin Mahon, who checked the questions and answers for accuracy. As it happens, I first met Martin at the reception where he collected his prize as the winner of my *In Dublin* film quiz many years ago.

Michael Dwyer

People Will Talk

QUESTIONS

Who, and in which movie, delivered these lines of dialogue:

Q1. 'Hang on a minute, lads. I've got a great idea.'

Q2. 'Mother's not feeling herself today.'

Q3. 'She loved Mozart and Bach. And the Beatles. And me.'

Q4. 'The last time I was inside a woman was when I visited the Statue of Liberty.'

Q5. 'So, which one of you gunslingers is going to ask me to dance?'

Q6. 'A live, freshly cut nerve is infinitely more sensitive.'

Q7. 'My taste includes both snails *and* oysters.'

Q8. 'Martha, will you show her where we keep the euphemism?

Q9. 'You can't fool me. There ain't no sanity clause.'

Q10. 'This is this.'

People Will Talk
ANSWERS

ANSWERS TO ROUND 1

A1. Michael Caine in *The Italian Job*

A2. Anthony Perkins in *Psycho*

A3. Woody Allen in *Crimes and Misdemeanors*

A4. Ryan O'Neal in *Love Story*

A5. Julia Roberts in *Michael Collins*

A6. Laurence Olivier in *Marathon Man*

A7. Laurence Olivier in *Spartacus*

A8. Richard Burton in *Who's Afraid of Virginia Woolf?*

A9. Chico Marx in *A Night at the Opera*

A10. Robert De Niro in *The Deer Hunter*

Irish Identity
QUESTIONS

Who played these real-life Irish people in the following movies?

Q1. Veronica Guerin in *Veronica Guerin* (2003)

Q2. James Joyce in *Nora* (2000)

Q3. Lady Gregory in *Young Cassidy* (1965)

Q4. Oscar Wilde in *Wilde* (1997)

Q5. Éamon de Valera in *Michael Collins* (1996)

Q6. Jonathan Swift in *Words upon the Window Pane* (1994)

Q7. Brendan Behan in *Borstal Boy* (2000)

Q8. Sean O'Casey in *Young Cassidy* (1965)

Q9. Charles Stewart Parnell in *Parnell* (1937)

Q10. George Best in *Best* (2000)

Irish Identity
ANSWERS

ANSWERS TO ROUND 2

A1. Cate Blanchett

A2. Ewan McGregor

A3. Edith Evans

A4. Stephen Fry

A5. Alan Rickman

A6. Jim Sheridan

A7. Shawn Hatosy

A8. Rod Taylor

A9. Clark Gable

A10. John Lynch

The Best of Youth
QUESTIONS

Q1. In 1958, Jack Nicholson made his film debut as what used to be known as a juvenile delinquent in a Roger Corman B-movie. What was its title?

Q2. In which 1971 drama did Daniel Day-Lewis make his film debut at the age of twelve, playing a schoolboy vandal?

Q3. Nominated for an Oscar in 2008, three months before her fourteenth birthday, this remarkably busy young actress made her screen debut in the RTÉ TV series *The Clinic* when she was nine. Who is she?

Q4. Tatum O'Neal was just ten when she won an Oscar for her performance as Addie Prayer in *Paper Moon* (1973). Name the future Oscar-winner who played the same role in the short-lived TV spin-off of that movie a year later.

Q5. She was eleven when Neil Jordan chose her to join his stellar cast in *Interview with the Vampire* (1994). She has featured in over forty movies since then, including a hit franchise in which she famously engaged in an upside-down kiss with the hero.

Q6. He was eleven when he made his film debut, co-starring with Susan Sarandon in *The Client* (1994). He featured in over twenty movies before his untimely death in 2008.

Q7. Arguably the definitive Brat Pack movie, *The Breakfast Club* (1986) brought five high school students together for detention. Molly Ringwald, Anthony Michael Hall and Judd Nelson played three of them. Who played the other two?

Q8. Name the 2004 body-swap comedy in which Jennifer Garner played a teen who wakes up as a woman more than twice her age.

The Best of Youth

QUESTIONS

Q9. Name the 1988 body-swap comedy in which Tom Hanks played a teen who wakes up as a man more than twice his age.

Q10. A prize-winner at Cannes in 2007, this award-winning animated feature charted the experiences of writer-director Marjane Satrapi growing up in Iran from the downfall of the Shah in 1978 through the Islamic Revolution. Name the film.

People Will Talk
ANSWERS

ANSWERS TO ROUND 3

A1. *Cry Baby Killer*

A2. *Sunday Bloody Sunday*

A3. Saoirse Ronan

A4. Jodie Foster

A5. Kirsten Dunst

A6. Brad Renfro

A7. Emilio Estevez and Ally Sheedy

A8. *13 Going on 30*

A9. *Big*

A10. *Persepolis*

Great Expectations
QUESTIONS

Which movies were publicised with the following slogans? The year of the original release date is given as a clue in each case.

Q1. 'In space no one can hear you scream' (1979)

Q2. 'It's time to kick some asteroid' (1998)

Q3. 'The coast is toast' (1997)

Q4. 'Who you gonna call?' (1984)

Q5. 'Garbo talks!' (1930)

Q6. 'Garbo laughs!' (1939)

Q7. 'The shadow of this woman darkened their love' (1940)

Q8. 'Get ready for rush hour' (1994)

Q9. 'The ultimate trip' (1968)

Q10. 'In space no one can hear you clean' (2008)

Great Expectations
ANSWERS

ANSWERS TO ROUND 4

A1. *Alien*

A2. *Armageddon*

A3. *Volcano*

A4. *Ghostbusters*

A5. *Anna Christie*

A6. *Ninotchka*

A7. *Rebecca*

A8. *Speed*

A9. *2001: A Space Odyssey*

A10. *WALL·E*

The Boys in the Band
QUESTIONS

Q1. Name the Beatle who wrote the score for *The Family Way* (1966).

Q2. Name the Beatle who wrote the score for *Wonderwall* (1968).

Q3. Name the Beatle whose company, HandMade Films, produced, among other films, *The Long Good Friday*, *Monty Python's Life of Brian*, *Time Bandits* and *Withnail & I*.

Q4. Name the song and the movie for which U2 received an Oscar nomination in the Best Original Song category.

Q5. Name the movie featuring a fictitious band whose members are David St Hubbins, Nigel Tufnel, Derek Smalls and Vic Savage.

Q6. Name the British guitarist who composed the score for *There Will Be Blood*, and name the band in which he plays.

Q7. Name the legendary guitarist who composed the scores for Michael Winner's less-than-legendary sequels, *Death Wish II* and *Death Wish 3*.

Q8. Name the pop group who starred in the musical fantasy *Head* (1968), on which Jack Nicholson shared the screenplay credit with director Bob Rafelson.

Q9. Name the former Kajagoogoo lead singer who had his biggest solo hit with the theme song from *The Neverending Story* (1984).

Q10. Name the German electronic band whose film scores include *Sorcerer* (1977), William Friedkin's remake of *The Wages of Fear*.

People Will Talk

ANSWERS

ANSWERS TO ROUND 5

A1. Paul McCartney

A2. George Harrison

A3. George Harrison

A4. *The Hands That Built America* (from *Gangs of New York*, 2002)

A5. *This is Spinal Tap*

A6. Jonny Greenwood (of Radiohead)

A7. Jimmy Page

A8. The Monkees

A9. Limahl

A10. Tangerine Dream

Work Is a Four-letter Word

QUESTIONS

What profession or position links each group of actors and their roles in these movies?

Q1. George Sanders *(All About Eve)*, Monty Woolley *(The Man Who Came to Dinner)*, David Niven *(Please Don't Eat the Daisies)*

Q2. Burt Lancaster *(Sweet Smell of Success)*, Rosalind Russell *(His Girl Friday)*, Gabriel Byrne *(Defence of the Realm)*

Q3. Winona Ryder *(Night on Earth)*, Jamie Foxx *(Collateral)*, Robert De Niro *(Jennifer on My Mind)*

Q4. Clint Eastwood *(Play Misty for Me)*, Jack Nicholson *(The King of Marvin Gardens)*, Jodie Foster *(The Brave One)*

Q5. Jodie Foster *(The Dangerous Lives of Altar Boys)*, Susan Sarandon *(Dead Man Walking)*, Deborah Kerr *(Black Narcissus)*

Q6. Rex Harrison *(The Agony and the Ecstasy)*, Anthony Quinn *(The Shoes of the Fishermen)*, Ringo Starr *(Lisztomania)*

Q7. Ralph Richardson *(The Fallen Idol)*, Anthony Hopkins *(The Remains of the Day)*, Alan Bates *(Gosford Park)*

Q8. Anne Bancroft *(The Miracle Worker)*, Peter O'Toole *(The Last Emperor)*, Jim Norton *(The Boy in the Striped Pyjamas)*

Q9. Maggie Gyllenhaal *(Stranger Than Fiction)*, Lyle Lovett *(Short Cuts)*, Colin Farrell *(A Home at the End of the World)*

Q10. Steve Coogan *(Marie Antoinette)*, Gregory Peck *(The Omen)*, Marlon Brando *(The Ugly American)*

Work Is a Four-letter Word
ANSWERS

ANSWERS TO ROUND 6

A1. Theatre critic

A2. Journalist

A3. Taxi driver (Of course, Robert De Niro also played the title role in *Taxi Driver*.)

A4. Radio-show presenter

A5. Nun (Deborah Kerr played another nun in *Heaven Knows Mr Allison*)

A6. Pope

A7. Butler

A8. Tutor

A9. Baker

A10. Ambassador

The Opposite of Sex

QUESTIONS

Who dressed as a member of the opposite sex in each of the following films?

Q1. *The Dark Knight* (2008)

Q2. *I'm Not There* (2007)

Q3. *Hairspray* (2007)

Q4. *Boys Don't Cry* (1999)

Q5. *Shakespeare in Love* (1998)

Q6. *Ed Wood* (1994)

Q7. *Glen or Glenda* (1953)

Q8. *Dressed to Kill* (1980)

Q9. *I Was a Male War Bride* (1949)

Q10. *Thunderbolt and Lightfoot* (1974)

The Opposite of Sex
ANSWERS

ANSWERS TO ROUND 7

A1. Heath Ledger

A2. Cate Blanchett

A3. John Travolta

A4. Hilary Swank

A5. Gwyneth Paltrow

A6. Johnny Depp

A7. Ed Wood

A8. Michael Caine

A9. Cary Grant

A10. Jeff Bridges

Power
QUESTIONS

Q1. Which former Irish government minister played himself in John Boorman's film *The General* (1998)?

Q2. Who played former US president Richard Nixon as an adult in *Nixon* (1995)?

Q3. Which English MP has received two Oscars for acting performances, and for which movies?

Q4. Which Oscar-winning actor was former US vice-president Al Gore's roommate at Harvard?

Q5. Which former president of France was the target of a fictional assassination attempt in the 1973 film of Frederick Forsyth's novel *The Day of the Jackal*?

Q6. Name the 1964 thriller featuring Ronald Reagan's last acting role before he became governor of California and president of the United States.

Q7. Which 1993 Wim Wenders movie featured former Russian premier Mikhail Gorbachev in a cameo as himself?

Q8. In which 1974 comedy did Peter Sellers play Adolf Hitler – and five other characters?

Q9. She was given a special Oscar in 1935, when she was only six years old, and was appointed as US ambassador to Ghana in 1974 and to Czechoslovakia in 1989. Name her.

Q10. Nine years before he became president of Poland, Lech Walesa appeared in a cameo as himself in a 1981 film that won the Palme d'Or at Cannes and was nominated for an Oscar. Name the film.

Power
ANSWERS

ANSWERS TO ROUND 8

A1. Des O'Malley

A2. Anthony Hopkins

A3. Glenda Jackson in *Women in Love* (1969) and *A Touch of Class* (1973)

A4. Tommy Lee Jones

A5. Charles de Gaulle

A6. *The Killers*

A7. *Far Away, So Close (In Weiter Ferne, So Nah!)*

A8. *Soft Beds, Hard Battles*

A9. Shirley Temple

A10. *Man of Iron (Czlowiek z Zelaza)*

Julie and Julia
QUESTIONS

Q1. Who played Julia in *Julia* (1977)?

Q2. Who was nominated for an Oscar for Best Actress for her performance in the title role of *Being Julia* (2004)?

Q3. Who played the leading roles as the three drag queens in the comedy road movie, *To Wong Foo Thanks for Everything, Julie Newmar* (1995)?

Q4. Who co-starred with Gabriel Byrne and Sting in *Julia and Julia* (1987)?

Q5. Who played Julia opposite Albert Brooks in *Defending Your Life* (1991)?

Q6. Which actress and singer played the title role in the 1956 thriller *Julie*?

Q7. Who played the title role in the comedy *Julia Misbehaves* (1948), six years after she won the Best Actress Oscar?

Q8. Who played the title role in the 1999 Mike Figgis film of the Strindberg play *Miss Julie*?

Q9. Which prolific French filmmaker and former critic directed *Céline and Julie Go Boating* (*Céline et Julie Vont en Bateau*, 1974)?

Q10. *Julie & Julia*, which was shot in 2008, was directed by Nora Ephron and features Amy Adams and Meryl Streep in the title roles. In which 1986 film, scripted by Ephron, did Streep play a character based on Ephron?

Julie and Julia

ANSWERS

ANSWERS TO ROUND 9

A1. Meryl Streep

A2. Annette Bening

A3. Wesley Snipes, Patrick Swayze and John Leguizamo

A4. Kathleen Turner

A5. Meryl Streep

A6. Doris Day

A7. Greer Garson

A8. Saffron Burrowes

A9. Jacques Rivette

A10. *Heartburn* (1986)

Couples
QUESTIONS

Q1. Their surnames were Parker and Barrow. Their first names provided the title of a classic 1967 movie. What is that title?

Q2. In *Melvin and Howard* (1980), Jason Robards played Howard, a real-life character who had directed two movies and produced many others. What's his surname?

Q3. Who played Thelma in *Thelma & Louise* (1991)?

Q4. Who played Withnail in *Withnail & I* (1987)?

Q5. To whom does 'Me' refer in the title of the documentary *Roger & Me* (1989)?

Q6. Who played W. C. Fields in *W. C. Fields and Me* (1976)?

Q7. Mia Farrow played Hannah in *Hannah and Her Sisters* (1986). Who played her two sisters?

Q8. George Segal and Jane Fonda played the title characters in this 1977 comedy. Jim Carrey and Téa Leoni played them in the 2005 remake of the same name. What's the title?

Q9. *Fat Man and Little Boy* (1989) featured Paul Newman and John Cusack. To what did the title refer?

Q10. The title roles of this 1970 spouse-swapping comedy were played by four actors who, in real life, had married and been divorced from other actors (France Nuyen, Robert Wagner, Barbra Streisand and Cary Grant). Name the movie and its four leading players.

Couples
ANSWERS

ANSWERS TO ROUND 10

A1. *Bonnie and Clyde*

A2. Howard Hughes

A3. Geena Davis

A4. Richard E. Grant

A5. The film's director, Michael Moore

A6. Rod Steiger

A7. Barbara Hershey and Dianne Wiest

A8. *Fun with Dick and Jane*

A9. The code names for the atomic bombs dropped on Nagasaki and Hiroshima in 1945

A10. *Bob & Carol & Ted & Alice* – played by Robert Culp, Natalie Wood, Elliott Gould and Dyan Cannon

Identity
QUESTIONS

Each of the following is a pseudonym used in screen credits – by whom in each case?

Q1. Bernard Shakey

Q2. Roderick Jaynes

Q3. Peter Andrews

Q4. Mary Ann Bernard

Q5. Arnold Crust (and Arnold Crust Jr)

Q6. Donald Kaufman

Q7. Leo Nichols

Q8. Ian McLellan Hunter

Q9. Robert Rich

Q10. P. H. Vazak

Identity
ANSWERS

ANSWERS TO ROUND 11

A1. Singer Neil Young for films he has directed

A2. Joel and Ethan Coen for their work as film editors on their movies

A3. Steven Soderbergh for his work as cinematographer on his own films

A4. Steven Soderbergh again, for his work as film editor on his movies

A5. Michael Winner, for his work as film editor on his movies

A6. Charlie Kaufman's fictional co-writer on his Oscar-nominated screenplay for *Adaptation* (2002)

A7. Ennio Morricone was credited under this name for his *Navajo Joe* (1966) score

A8. Dalton Trumbo, who was blacklisted at the time, used this name as a front on his Oscar-winning screenplay for *Roman Holiday* (1953)

A9. Dalton Trumbo again, who was still on the blacklist when he used this name as a front on his second Oscar-winning screenplay, *The Brave One* (1956)

A10. Robert Towne experienced 'creative difficulties' on *Greystoke: The Legend of Tarzan, Lord of the Apes* (1984) – and he used his sheepdog's name for his credit on the screenplay (which earned him an Oscar nomination)

Things Change

QUESTIONS

By which professional name is each of the following actors better known?

Q1. Derek Jules Gaspard Ulric Niven van den Bogaerde

Q2. Doris Mary Ann von Kappelhoff

Q3. Issur Danielovitch Demsky

Q4. Philip John Clapp

Q5. Susan Abigail Tomalin

Q6. Ramón Estévez

Q7. Harlean Carpentier

Q8. Charles Buchinsky

Q9. Timothy Allen Dick

Q10. Vladimir Palanuik

Things Change
ANSWERS

ANSWERS TO ROUND 12

A1. Dirk Bogarde

A2. Doris Day

A3. Kirk Douglas

A4. Johnny Knoxville

A5. Susan Sarandon

A6. Martin Sheen

A7. Jean Harlow

A8. Charles Bronson

A9. Tim Allen

A10. Jack Palance

The Hours
QUESTIONS

Q1. Glenn Ford and Van Helfin took this train in 1957. Christian Bale and Russell Crowe took it in 2007. What's the title common to both movies?

Q2. Spike Lee's 2002 New York crime drama starred Edward Norton and Philip Seymour Hoffman. Name it.

Q3. The time in the title is much shorter than this 2001 movie with Robert De Niro as a homicide detective, Edward Burns as an arson investigator and Kelsey Grammer as the host of a sleazy TV show. What is the title?

Q4. The title of this 2002 thriller refers to the area of a shopping centre where the central character, a stalker creepily played by Robin Williams, is employed. Name the film.

Q5. Name the renowned country singer who made his cinema debut as a criminal who uses a six-year-old (played by Ron Howard) as a human shield in the low-budget 1961 crime drama *Five Minutes to Live*.

Q6. *Nine Hours to Rama* (1963) featured Horst Buchholz (from *The Magnificent Seven*) as the assassin of a man who would become the subject of an Oscar-winning biopic. Name that biopic.

Q7. Martin Scorsese's 1985 black comedy set over one night in New York featured Griffin Dunne and Rosanna Arquette. Name the movie.

Q8. Max von Sydow, as the French foreign minister, and Roman Polanski, as a sadistic Paris police inspector, injected some vitality into this tired 2007 sequel to an action-comedy. Name the film.

The Hours

QUESTIONS

Q9. Nicolas Cage leads a gang of thieves on a mission to steal fifty cars over a single night in this big-budget 2000 remake of a low-budget 1974 movie. What's the title common to both films?

Q10. Max von Sydow played a disturbed painter with Liv Ullmann as his pregnant wife in Ingmar Bergman's 1968 Gothic horror film. The original title was *Vargtimmen* (which is helpful only if you speak Swedish). By what title was it released here?

The Hours

ANSWERS

ANSWERS TO ROUND 13

A1. *3:10 to Yuma*

A2. *The 25th Hour*

A3. *15 Minutes*

A4. *One Hour Photo*

A5. Johnny Cash

A6. *Gandhi*

A7. *After Hours*

A8. *Rush Hour 3*

A9. *Gone in 60 Seconds*

A10. *Hour of the Wolf*

Great Expectations
QUESTIONS

Which movies were publicised with the following slogans? The year of the original release date is given as a clue in each case.

Q1. 'On every street in every city, there's a nobody who dreams of being a somebody' (1976)

Q2. 'His whole life was a million-to-one shot' (1976)

Q3. 'The story of a man who was too proud to run' (1952)

Q4. 'The true story of a real fake' (2002)

Q5. 'His love is real. But he is not.' (2001)

Q6. 'His story will touch you, even though he can't' (1990)

Q7. 'He's the only kid ever to get into trouble before he was born' (1985)

Q8. 'Don't get him wet, keep him out of bright light, and never feed him after midnight' (1982)

Q9. 'Just when you thought it was safe to go back in the water' (1978)

Q10. 'Bigger, better, more absorbent' (2004)

Great Expectations
ANSWERS

ANSWERS TO ROUND 14

A1. *Taxi Driver*

A2. *Rocky*

A3. *High Noon*

A4. *Catch Me If You Can*

A5. *A.I.*

A6. *Edward Scissorhands*

A7. *Back to the Future*

A8. *Gremlins*

A9. *Jaws 2*

A10. *The SpongeBob SquarePants Movie*

The Emerald Forest

QUESTIONS

Q1. What Irish landmark provided an essential location for, among other movies, *The Italian Job*, *McVicar* and *The Escapist*?

Q2. His mother is from Longford. He is named after two Irish saints. His middle name is Colmcille. Name the Oscar-winning director.

Q3. Pig, Kitten and Scarecrow are among the roles played by this versatile actor from Cork. Name him.

Q4. Name this Oscar-winning director whose early movies in the 1960s included *Dementia 13* (also known as *The Haunted and the Hunted*), which was shot in Ireland, and the stage-Irish musical *Finian's Rainbow*.

Q5. In the history of the Cannes Film Festival, only one Irish thespian has ever received the award for Best Actor or Best Actress. Who, and for what film?

Q6. Who played the father of Christy Brown in Jim Sheridan's 1989 film *My Left Foot?*

Q7. And who played Christy as a boy in that film?

Q8. All bar one of these movies was shot partly or in full in Ireland: *The Spy Who Came in From the Cold*, *Becoming Jane*, *Reign of Fire* and *Waking Ned*. Which one was not?

Q9. Which Hollywood movie star was named in the title of Thaddeus O'Sullivan's BAFTA-nominated 1985 short film based on a Sean Ó Faoláin story and featuring Brenda Fricker and Bob Hoskins?

Q10. Mickey Rourke played a guilt-riddled IRA bomber in this 1987 melodrama, which was selected to open the London Film Festival and then controversially withdrawn. Name the film.

The Emerald Forest
ANSWERS

ANSWERS TO ROUND 15

A1. Kilmainham Jail

A2. Mel Gibson

A3. Cillian Murphy, in *Disco Pigs, Breakfast on Pluto* and *Batman Begins*

A4. Francis Ford Coppola

A5. Richard Harris for *This Sporting Life* (1963)

A6. Ray McAnally

A7. Hugh O'Conor

A8. *Waking Ned*, which was set in Ireland but shot on the Isle of Man

A9. Clark Gable, in *The Woman Who Married Clark Gable*

A10. *A Prayer Before Dying*

Tiresome
QUESTIONS

Q1. This busy actor has starred in the twenty-first-century remakes of *Alfie*, *Sleuth* and *All the King's Men*. Who is he?

Q2. Name the movie in which the screaming heroine was played in different versions by Fay Wray (in 1933), Jessica Lange (in 1976) and Naomi Watts (in 2005).

Q3. *The Taking of Pelham 123* (1974), *Silver Streak* (1976), *The Darjeeling Limited* (2007). To what mode of transport do all three movie titles refer?

Q4. He died in 1967 and subsequently was portrayed in different movies by Omar Sharif, Gael Garcia Bernal and Benicio Del Toro. Who is he?

Q5. The same fictional sleuth has been played by, among others, Robert Duvall, Dudley Moore and Joanne Woodward in different movies. Who?

Q6. This fictional sleuth has been played by, among others, Tony Randall, Albert Finney and Peter Ustinov in different movies. Who?

Q7. This fictional character has been played by, among others, Lon Chaney (in 1922), Alec Guinness (in 1948), and Ben Kingsley (in 2005). Who?

Q8. What international event provides the setting for *Walk Don't Run* (1966), *Chariots of Fire* (1981) and *Munich* (2005)?

Q9. In addition to directing and producing, Clint Eastwood, John Carpenter and Mike Figgis have provided what other important element in some or many of their movies (and the answer isn't acting or screenwriting)?

Q10. This notorious criminal has been portrayed by many actors, including Jason Robards, Ben Gazzara and Robert De Niro. Who?

Tiresome

ANSWERS

ANSWERS TO ROUND 16

A1. Jude Law

A2. *King Kong*

A3. Trains

A4. Che Guevara: played by Omar Sharif in *Che!*, Gael Garcia Bernal in *The Motorcycle Diaries*, and Benicio Del Toro in *Che*

A5. Dr Watson: played by Robert Duvall in *The 7% Solution*, Dudley Moore in *The Hound of the Baskervilles*, and Joanne Woodward in *They Might Be Giants*

A6. Hercule Poirot: played by Tony Randall in *The Alphabet Murders*, Albert Finney in *Murder on the Orient Express*, and Peter Ustinov in *Death on the Nile*, *Evil Under the Sun* and *Appointment with Death*

A7. Fagin, in different versions of *Oliver Twist*

A8. The Olympic Games

A9. All three have composed the music score for some or all of their movies.

A10. Al Capone, played by Jason Robards in *The St Valentine's Day Massacre* (1967), Ben Gazzara in *Capone* (1975) and Robert De Niro in *The Untouchables* (1987)

The Singer Not the Song
QUESTIONS

Q1. Which movie features Colin Farrell singing *I Fought the Law* on the soundtrack?

Q2. Name the musical in which Clint Eastwood performs *I Talk to the Trees*.

Q3. In which movie does Mick Jagger sing *The Wild Colonial Boy*?

Q4. Name the movie in which Heath Ledger serenades Julia Stiles with his rendition of *Can't Take My Eyes Off You*

Q5. In which Oirish musical does Petula Clark trill 'How Are Things in Glocca Morra?'?

Q6. In which movie did Jack Nicholson adopt a deliberately Oirish accent to sing a verse of *Mother Macree*?

Q7. This busy actress took time out to record the 2008 album *Anywhere I Lay My Head*, consisting mostly of Tom Waits covers. Who is she?

Q8. In which movie did Edward Norton croon the standard 'My Baby Just Cares for Me'?

Q9. This action-movie performer demonstrated his singing voice with his band, Thunderbox, on the 2006 album *Mojo Priest*. It featured covers of blues standards and his original compositions 'Alligator Ass' and 'Talk to My Ass'. Identify this man of so many talents.

Q10. Name the four actors who played the Beatles in *Walk Hard: The Dewey Cox Story* (2007).

The Singer Not the Song
ANSWERS

ANSWERS TO ROUND 17

A1. *Intermission*

A2. *Paint Your Wagon*

A3. *Ned Kelly*

A4. *10 Things I Hate About You*

A5. *Finian's Rainbow*

A6. *The Departed*

A7. Scarlett Johansson

A8. *Everyone Says I Love You*

A9. Steven Seagal

A10. Paul Rudd (as John Lennon), Jack Black (Paul McCartney), Justin Long (George Harrison) and Jason Schwartzman (Ringo Starr)

Animal Crackers

QUESTIONS

What type of animal is each of the following title character?

Q1. *Bambi* (1942)

Q2. *Babe* (1995)

Q3. *Beethoven* (1992)

Q4. *Seabiscuit* (2003)

Q5. *Dumbo* (1941)

Q6. Tonto in *Harry and Tonto* (1974)

Q7. Oliver in *Oliver & Company* (1988)

Q8. *Ben* (1972)

Q9. *Bolt* (2008)

Q10. *Harvey* (1950)

Animal Crackers
ANSWERS

ANSWERS TO ROUND 18

A1. A deer

A2. A pig

A3. A dog

A4. A horse

A5. An elephant

A6. A cat

A7. A cat

A8. A rat

A9. A dog

A10. A rabbit (a six-foot invisible rabbit)

Michael Dwyer's Film Quiz Book
Irish, Hollywood and World Cinema

Parenthood

QUESTIONS

Q1. Who played the parents of the Ben Stiller character in the *Meet the Parents* sequel *Meet the Fockers* (2004)?

Q2. A blond Colin Farrell played the title role in *Alexander* (2004). Who played his mother, Olympias?

Q3. In the 1962 version of *The Manchurian Candidate*, she played the mother of the character played by Laurence Harvey – even though she was only two years older than Harvey. Who is she?

Q4. Who played the eponymous father in the 1991 French film *Mon Père, Ce Héros* – and reprised the role in the 1994 US remake, *My Father, The Hero*?

Q5. Who played the homely but homicidal mother at the centre of the 1994 John Waters comedy *Serial Mom*?

Q6. Who played the mother of the overweight teen at the centre of *Hairspray*, the 2007 musical remake based on the 1988 John Waters comedy of the same name?

Q7. Who played the father of the Faye Dunaway character in *Chinatown* (1974) – and, it transpired, the father of her daughter?

Q8. Name the Hollywood star portrayed as a selfish, domineering matriarch by Faye Dunaway in *Mommie Dearest* (1981)?

Q9. Name the Hollywood star who played the selfless, doting and much-suffering mother who was the title character in the classic 1945 melodrama *Mildred Pierce*.

Q10. In Matt Clark's 1988 film *Da*, based on Hugh Leonard's stage play, Barnard Hughes played the title role. Who played his son, a US-based Irish playwright?

Parenthood
ANSWERS

ANSWERS TO ROUND 19

A1. Barbra Streisand and Dustin Hoffman

A2. Angelina Jolie

A3. Angela Lansbury

A4. Gérard Depardieu

A5. Kathleen Turner

A6. John Travolta

A7. John Huston

A8. Joan Crawford

A9. Joan Crawford

A10. Martin Sheen

The Neon Bible

QUESTIONS

Q1. It has been said that film directors like to play God, but some actors actually have played God. Who had the role in *Bruce Almighty* (2003) and its sequel, *Evan Almighty* (2007)?

Q2. . . . and who played the title role in *Oh, God!* (1977)?

Q3. Who played Jesus in *The Greatest Story Ever Told* (1965)?

Q4. . . . and in *The Last Temptation of Christ* (1988)?

Q5. . . . and in *The Passion of the Christ* (2004)?

Q6. In John Huston's *The Bible: In the Beginning* (1966), who played Adam?

Q7. . . . and who played Cain in the same film?

Q8. Which celebrated Irish actress played Mary in Nicholas Ray's Biblical epic *King of Kings* (1961)?

Q9. . . . and which late US actor (and longtime Cork resident) played Pontius Pilate in that film?

Q10. David McCallum, Rip Torn and Harvey Keitel have played this Biblical character in different movies. Who, and in which films?

The Neon Bible
ANSWERS

ANSWERS TO ROUND 20

A1. Morgan Freeman

A2. George Burns

A3. Max von Sydow

A4. Willem Dafoe

A5. Jim Caviezel

A6. Michael Parks

A7. Richard Harris

A8. Siobhán McKenna

A9. Hurd Hatfield

A10. Judas Iscariot, played by David McCallum in *The Greatest Story Ever Told* (1965), Rip Torn in *King of Kings* (1961) and Harvey Keitel in *The Last Temptation of Christ* (1998)

Once Upon a Time in America
QUESTIONS

**The following US releases had different titles on this side of
the Atlantic. In each case, give the title under which they
were released in Ireland and Britain.**

Q1. *Harry Potter and the Sorcerer's Stone* (2001)

Q2. *Live Free or Die Hard* (2007)

Q3. *La Femme Nikita* (1990)

Q4. *Hoosiers* (1986)

Q5. *The Longest Yard* (1974)

Q6. *Out of the Past* (1947)

Q7. *Rory O'Shea Was Here* (2004)

Q8. *The Fortune Cookie* (1966)

Q9. *Young Scarface* (1947)

Q10. *Stairway to Heaven* (1946)

Once Upon a Time in America
ANSWERS

ANSWERS TO ROUND 21

A1. *Harry Potter and the Philosopher's Stone*

A2. *Die Hard 4.0*

A3. *Nikita*

A4. *Best Shot*

A5. *The Mean Machine*

A6. *Build My Gallows High*

A7. *Inside I'm Dancing*

A8. *Meet Whiplash Willie*

A9. *Brighton Rock*

A10. *A Matter of Life and Death*

The Letter
QUESTIONS

Who played the title roles in the following films?

Q1. *W.* (2008)

Q2. *W.W. and the Dixie Dancekings* (1975)

Q3. *John Q* (2002)

Q4. *McQ* (1974)

Q5. *Madame X* (1966)

Q6. *Cecil B DeMented* (2000)

Q7. *The Story of Adèle H./L'Histoire d'Adèle H.* (1975)

Q8. *Boy A* (2007)

Q9. *Dr T and the Women* (2000)

Q10. *The 5,000 Fingers of Dr T* (1953)

The Letter
ANSWERS

ANSWERS TO ROUND 22

A1. Josh Brolin

A2. Burt Reynolds

A3. Denzel Washington

A4. John Wayne

A5. Lana Turner

A6. Stephen Dorff

A7. Isabelle Adjani

A8. Andrew Garfield

A9. Richard Gere

A10. Hans Conried

Missing
QUESTIONS

What is the missing word in these unusually long movie titles? The films' directors and release dates are in brackets.

Q1. *Indiana Jones and the ___ of the Crystal Skull* (Steven Spielberg, 2008)

Q2. *The Assassination of Jesse James by the ___ Robert Ford* (Andrew Dominik, 2007)

Q3. *Women on the ___ of a Nervous Breakdown* (Pedro Almódovar, 1988)

Q4. *Talladega Nights: The ___ of Ricky Bobby* (Adam McKay, 2006)

Q5. *Everything You Always Wanted to Know About ___ But Were Afraid to Ask* (Woody Allen, 1972)

Q6. *Dr Strangelove or: How I Learned to Stop ___ and Love the Bomb* (Stanley Kubrick, 1964)

Q7. *The Fearless ___ Killers, Or Pardon Me, Your Teeth are in My Neck* (Roman Polanski, 1967)

Q8. *Borat: Cultural Learnings of America for Make ___ Glorious Nation of Kazakhstan* (2006)

Q9. *The ___ Who Went Up a Hill But Came Down a Mountain* (Christopher Monger, 1995)

Q10. *The Effect of Gamma Rays on Man-in-the-Moon ___* (Paul Newman, 1972)

Missing

ANSWERS

ANSWERS TO ROUND 23

A1. Kingdom *(Indiana Jones and the Kingdom of the Crystal Skull)*

A2. Coward *(The Assassination of Jesse James by the Coward Robert Ford)*

A3. Verge *(Women on the Verge of a Nervous Breakdown)*

A4. Ballad *(Talladega Nights: The Ballad of Ricky Bobby)*

A5. Sex *(Everything You Always Wanted to Know About Sex But Were Afraid to Ask)*

A6. Worrying *(Dr Strangelove or: How I Learned to Stop Worrying and Love the Bomb)*

A7. Vampire *(The Fearless Vampire Killers, Or Pardon Me, Your Teeth are in My Neck)*

A8. Benefit *(Borat: Cultural Learnings of America for Make Benefit Glorious Nation of Kazakhstan)*

A9. Englishman *(The Englishman Who Went Up a Hill But Came Down a Mountain)*

A10. Marigolds *(The Effect of Gamma Rays on Man-in-the-Moon Marigolds)*

Great Expectations
QUESTIONS

Which movies were publicised with the following slogans? The year of the original release date is given as a clue in each case.

Q1. 'Does for rock and roll what *The Sound of Music* did for hills' (1984)

Q2. 'You won't believe your eye' (2001)

Q3. 'This is Benjamin. He's a little worried about his future.' (1968)

Q4. 'The future of law enforcement' (1987)

Q5. 'A tale of murder, lust, greed, revenge, and seafood' (1988)

Q6. 'Five criminals. One line-up. No coincidences.' (1995)

Q7. 'Fear can hold you prisoner. Hope can set you free.' (1994)

Q8. 'One man's struggle to take it easy' (1986)

Q9. 'There's something about your first piece' (1999)

Q10. 'Get a grip on yourself' (1994)

Great Expectations
ANSWERS

ANSWERS TO ROUND 24

A1. *This is Spinal Tap*

A2. *Monsters, Inc.*

A3. *The Graduate*

A4. *RoboCop*

A5. *A Fish Called Wanda*

A6. *The Usual Suspects*

A7. *The Shawshank Redemption*

A8. *Ferris Bueller's Day Off*

A9. *American Pie*

A10. *Spanking the Monkey*

This Sporting Life
QUESTIONS

Name the competitive sport featured in each of the following films:

Q1. *This Sporting Life* (1963)

Q2. *Chariots of Fire* (1981)

Q3. *When Saturday Comes* (1996)

Q4. *Any Given Sunday* (1999)

Q5. *Breaking Away* (1978)

Q6. *Body and Soul* (1947)

Q7. *Slap Shot* (1977)

Q8. *National Velvet* (1944)

Q9. *Tin Cup* (1996)

Q10. *Balls of Fury* (2007)

This Sporting Life
ANSWERS

ANSWERS TO ROUND 25

A1. Rugby

A2. Running

A3. Soccer

A4. American football

A5. Cycling

A6. Boxing

A7. Ice hockey

A8. Horse racing

A9. Golf

A10. Table tennis

Loose Connections
QUESTIONS

Q1. Name the Irish actor who is the connection between Duran Duran and *Ulysses*

Q2. Which movie title connects Whoopi Goldberg and the Rolling Stones?

Q3. Mark O'Halloran, John Lynch and Michael Fassbender have all played this Irishman, whose death in 1981 was covered extensively in the international media. Who is he, and in which films did those actors portray him?

Q4. Which US actor has a common link with these French films: *À Bout de Souffle* (1960), *La Femme Infidèle* (1968), *Les Choses de la Vie* (1969), *Le Retour de Martin Guerre* (1982).

Q5. Name the literary adaptation filmed in 1955 and 1999 that connects Deborah Kerr, Julianne Moore and Sarah Miles.

Q6. What number connects Anthony Hopkins, Uma Thurman, Scarlett Johansson and Eminem, and why?

Q7. Of the thirteen feature films made by Joel and Ethan Coen, ten have been based on their original screenplays. Name their two films adapted from other sources.

Q8. What is the literary source that connects the titles of Peter Ormrod's 1986 Irish film, *Eat the Peach*, and Patricia Rozema's 1987 Canadian film, *I've Heard the Mermaids Singing?*

Q9. In what noble profession did François Truffaut, Eric Rohmer, Paul Schrader and Peter Bogdanovich work before they directed films?

Q10. What rare distinction is shared by film directors Jean-Pierre and Luc Dardenne, Emir Kusturica, Shohei Imamura, Bille August and Francis Ford Coppola?

Loose Connections

ANSWERS

ANSWERS TO ROUND 26

A1. Milo O'Shea, who played a character named Duran Duran in *Barbarella* and Leopold Bloom in *Ulysses*

A2. *Jumpin' Jack Flash*

A3. Bobby Sands: played by Mark O'Halloran in *H3* (2001), John Lynch in *Some Mother's Son* (1996) and Michael Fassbender in *Hunger* (2008)

A4. Richard Gere starred in the US remakes of all four films: respectively, *Breathless*, *Unfaithful*, *Intersection* and *Somersby*

A5. *The End of the Affair*: one of the two principal characters is named Sarah Miles, who was played by Deborah Kerr in the 1955 version and by Julianne Moore in 1999

A6. All four feature in films with the same number in the title: Anthony Hopkins in *When Eight Bells Toll* (1971), Uma Thurman in *Jennifer Eight* (1992), Scarlett Johansson in *Eight Legged Freaks* (2002) and Eminem in *8 Mile* (2002)

A7. *The Ladykillers* (2004), based on William Rose's screenplay for the original 1955 film version, and *No Country for Old Men* (2007), adapted from the novel by Cormac McCarthy

A8. Both titles are taken from T. S. Eliot's poem 'The Love Song of J. Alfred Prufrock'

A9. All four were film critics

A10. They are the only two-time winners of the Palme d'Or for best feature film at the Cannes Film Festival: the Dardennes with *Rosetta* and *L'enfant*, Kusturica with *When Father Was Away on Business* and *Underground*, Imamura with *The Ballad of Narayama* and *The Eel*, August with *Pelle the Conqueror* and *The Best Intentions* and Coppola with *The Conversation* and *Apocalypse Now*

Coming Home
QUESTIONS

In which country was each of the following actors born?

Q1. Mel Gibson

Q2. Russell Crowe

Q3. Guy Pearce

Q4. Nicole Kidman

Q5. Naomi Watts

Q6. Jim Carrey

Q7. Keanu Reeves

Q8. Liv Ullmann

Q9. Laurence Harvey

Q10. Edward G. Robinson

Coming Home
ANSWERS

ANSWERS TO ROUND 27

A1. US (New York)

A2. New Zealand

A3. England

A4. US (Hawaii)

A5. England

A6. Lebanon

A7. Canada

A8. Tokyo

A9. Lithuania

A10. Romania

Imitation of Life
QUESTIONS

Who played the following?

Q1. Charles Chaplin in *Chaplin* (1992)

Q2. Bela Lugosi in *Ed Wood* (1994)

Q3. Joan Crawford in *Mommie Dearest* (1981)

Q4. Britt Ekland in *The Life and Death of Peter Sellers* (2004)

Q5. Katharine Hepburn in *The Aviator* (2004)

Q6. Errol Flynn in *The Aviator* (2004)

Q7. Errol Flynn in *Flynn* (1996)

Q8. Rudolph Valentino in *Valentino* (1977)

Q9. Lon Chaney in *Man of a Thousand Faces* (1957)

Q10. Charles Chaplin in *The Cat's Meow* (2001)

Imitation of Life
ANSWERS

ANSWERS TO ROUND 28

A1. Robert Downey Jr

A2. Martin Landau

A3. Faye Dunaway

A4. Charlize Theron

A5. Cate Blanchett

A6. Jude Law

A7. Guy Pearce

A8. Rudolf Nureyev

A9. James Cagney

A10. Eddie Izzard

State of Play

QUESTIONS

Name the William Shakespeare plays which inspired or provided the basis for the following films.

Q1. *O* (2001)

Q2. *10 Things I Hate About You* (1999)

Q3. *Prospero's Books* (1991)

Q4. *My Own Private Idaho* (1991)

Q5. *Ran* (1985)

Q6. *Kiss Me, Kate* (1953)

Q7. *Forbidden Planet* (1956)

Q8. *My Kingdom* (2001)

Q9. *Catch My Soul* (1974)

Q10. *Throne of Blood/Kumonosu Jo* (1957)

State of Play
ANSWERS

ANSWERS TO ROUND 29

A1. *Othello*

A2. *The Taming of the Shrew*

A3. *The Tempest*

A4. *Henry IV, Part 1*

A5. *King Lear*

A6. *The Taming of the Shrew*

A7. *The Tempest*

A8. *King Lear*

A9. *Othello*

A10. *Macbeth*

Remember My Name
QUESTIONS

By which professional name is each of the following actors better known?

Q1. Rudolfo Pietro Filberto Raffaello Guglielmi di Valentina

Q2. Maureen FitzSimons

Q3. Maurice Micklewhite

Q4. Julie Anne Smith

Q5. Lee Jun Fan

Q6. Lucille Fay LeSueur

Q7. Margarita Carmen Cansino

Q8. Mavis Fluck

Q9. James Stewart (and the answer is not 'James Stewart')

Q10. Michael Douglas (and the answer is not 'Michael Douglas')

Remember My Name
ANSWERS

ANSWERS TO ROUND 30

A1. Rudolph Valentino

A2. Maureen O'Hara

A3. Michael Caine

A4. Julianne Moore

A5. Bruce Lee

A6. Joan Crawford

A7. Rita Hayworth

A8. Diana Dors

A9. Stewart Granger

A10. Michael Keaton

Rent
QUESTIONS

Q1. Who won the first of her two Oscars as call-girl Gloria Wandrous in a 1961 drama?

Q2. Who won the first of two Oscars as call-girl Bree Daniels in a 1971 thriller?

Q3. Who, in 1969, played hustler Joe Buck – and received the first of his four Oscar nominations?

Q4. Who, in 1976, at the age of thirteen, played a prostitute – and received the first of her four Oscar nominations?

Q5. In which 1991 film did River Phoenix and Keanu Reeves play prostitutes bonding in Portland, Oregon?

Q6. Who played a bored Parisian turning to prostitution in the afternoons in *Belle de Jour* (1967)?

Q7. Who played the title role in *American Gigolo* (1980)?

Q8. The star of *American Gigolo* turned to paying client in a glossily sanitised 1990 romantic comedy. What was that movie, and who played the prostitute?

Q9. Name the Neil Jordan film in which Cathy Tyson played a prostitute with Bob Hoskins as her driver and minder.

Q10. Who directed *Flesh* (1968) and *Forty Deuce* (1982), in which Joe Dallesandro and Kevin Bacon, respectively, played prostitutes?

Rent
ANSWERS

ANSWERS TO ROUND 31

A1. Elizabeth Taylor (in *BUtterfield 8*)

A2. Jane Fonda (in *Klute*)

A3. Jon Voight (in *Midnight Cowboy*)

A4. Jodie Foster (in *Taxi Driver*)

A5. *My Own Private Idaho*

A6. Catherine Deneuve

A7. Richard Gere

A8. *Pretty Woman*, Julia Roberts

A9. *Mona Lisa*

A10. Paul Morrissey

Adaptation.
QUESTIONS

Who wrote the novels – or novellas or short stories – on which these movies are based?

Q1. *Rebecca* (1940)

Q2. *Stand By Me* (1986)

Q3. *1408* (2007)

Q4. *Don't Look Now* (1973)

Q5. *Breakfast at Tiffany's* (1961)

Q6. *The Informer* (1935)

Q7. *Clueless* (1995)

Q8. *Away From Her* (2007)

Q9. *Gigi* (1958)

Q10. *Young Frankenstein* (1974)

Adaptation.
ANSWERS

ANSWERS TO ROUND 32

A1. Daphne Du Maurier

A2. Stephen King

A3. Stephen King

A4. Daphne Du Maurier

A5. Truman Capote

A6. Liam O'Flaherty

A7. Jane Austen (the film is based on *Emma*)

A8. Alice Munro (the story is 'The Bear Went Over the Mountain')

A9. Colette

A10. Mary Shelley

The Group
QUESTIONS

Each of the following groups features actors who have played the same characters in different movies. In each group, name the character that connects the actors.

Q1. James Garner, Humphrey Bogart and Robert Mitchum

Q2. John Huston, Edward Fox and Judi Dench

Q3. Gerard Butler, Gary Oldman and George Hamilton

Q4. Marianne Faithfull, Jean Simmons and Kate Winslet

Q5. Guy Pearce, David Bowie and Crispin Glover

Q6. Telly Savalas, David Bowie and Michael Palin

Q7. Natalie Portman, Merle Oberon and Vanessa Redgrave

Q8. Roger Daltrey, Julian Sands and Dirk Bogarde

Q9. Bette Davis, Glenda Jackson and Quentin Crisp

Q10. Alain Delon, Dennis Hopper and Matt Damon

The Group
ANSWERS

ANSWERS TO ROUND 33

A1. Philip Marlowe: played by James Garner in *Marlowe* (1969), Humphrey Bogart in *The Big Sleep* (1946) and Robert Mitchum in both *Farewell, My Lovely* (1975) and *The Big Sleep* (1978)

A2. M: played by John Huston in *Casino Royale* (1967), Edward Fox in *Never Say Never Again* (1983) and Judi Dench in *GoldenEye* (1995) and the next five James Bond films

A3. Dracula: played by Gerard Butler in *Dracula 2000* (2000), Gary Oldman in *Bram Stoker's Dracula* (1992) and George Hamilton in *Love at First Bite* (1979)

A4. Ophelia: played by Marianne Faithfull in *Hamlet* (1969), Jean Simmons in *Hamlet* (1948) and Kate Winslet in *Hamlet* (1996)

A5. Andy Warhol: played by Guy Pearce in *Factory Girl* (2006), David Bowie in *Basquiat* (1996) and Crispin Glover in *The Doors* (1991)

A6. Pontius Pilate: played by Telly Savalas in *The Greatest Story Ever Told* (1965), David Bowie in *The Last Temptation of Christ* (1988) and Michael Palin in *Monty Python's Life of Brian* (1979)

A7. Anne Boleyn: played by Natalie Portman in *The Other Boleyn Girl* (2007), Merle Oberon in *The Private Life of Henry VIII* (1933) and Vanessa Redgrave in *A Man For All Seasons* (1966)

The Group
ANSWERS

A8. Franz Liszt: played by Roger Daltrey in *Lisztomania* (1975), Julian Sands in *Impromptu* (1991) and Dirk Bogarde in *Song Without End* (1960)

A9. Queen Elizabeth I: played by Bette Davis in both *The Private Lives of Elizabeth and Essex* (1939) and *The Virgin Queen* (1955), Glenda Jackson in *Mary, Queen of Scots* (1971) and Quentin Crisp in *Orlando* (1992)

A10. Tom Ripley: played by Alain Delon in *Plein Soleil* (1960), Dennis Hopper in *The American Friend* (1977) and Matt Damon in *The Talented Mr Ripley* (1999)

Great Expectations

QUESTIONS

Which movies were publicised with the following slogans? The year of the original release date is given as a clue in each case.

Q1. 'They're young . . . they're in love . . . and they kill people.' (1967)

Q2. 'In 1959 a lot of people were killing time. Kit and Holly were killing people.' (1973)

Q3. 'Where were you in '62?' (1973)

Q4. 'History is about to be rewritten by two guys who can't spell.' (1989)

Q5. 'This is the weekend they didn't play golf.' (1972)

Q6. 'Man is the warmest place to hide!' (1982)

Q7. 'Love is in the hair.' (1998)

Q8. 'I drink your milkshake.' (2007)

Q9. 'It's still the same old story, a fight for love and glory.' (1972)

Q10. 'From the brother of the director of *Ghost.*' (1994)

Great Expectations

ANSWERS

ANSWERS TO ROUND 35

A1. *Bonnie and Clyde*

A2. *Badlands*

A3. *American Graffiti*

A4. *Bill & Ted's Excellent Adventure*

A5. *Deliverance*

A6. *The Thing*

A7. *There's Something About Mary*

A8. *There Will be Blood*

A9. *Play It Again, Sam*

A10. *The Naked Gun 33 1/3: The Final Insult*

The Four Seasons

QUESTIONS

Brief outlines follow for movies featuring one of the four seasons in the title. In each case, identify the film.

Q1. Ryan Phillippe, Sarah Michelle Gellar and Anne Heche feature in a hit horror-thriller that spawned a sequel with an extra word in the title.

Q2. Tensions rise when a notorious serial killer is on the loose in New York City in Spike Lee's 1977-set movie featuring John Leguizamo, Adrien Brody and Mira Sorvino.

Q3. Shot in Ireland, this historical drama won Katharine Hepburn the third of her four Oscars and marked the feature-film debut of Anthony Hopkins.

Q4. Elizabeth Taylor, Katharine Hepburn and Montgomery Clift star in Gore Vidal's adaptation of a Tennessee Williams play.

Q5. An actress (Vivien Leigh) falls for a younger man (Warren Beatty) in this Tennessee Williams adaptation. (Helen Mirren and Olivier Martinez played those characters in a later US TV version filmed in Ireland.)

Q6. David Lean directs Katherine Hepburn as a lonely American falling in love after a brief encounter in Venice.

Q7. Richard Gere falls for a terminally ill younger woman played by Winona Ryder.

Q8. John Ford's western featuring Richard Widmark, Carroll Baker, Sal Mineo and Karl Malden.

Q9. Ingmar Bergman directs Ingrid Bergman in an emotionally raw family drama that earned Oscar nominations for both Bergmans.

Q10. A political-conspiracy satire with an eclectic cast including Jeff Bridges, John Huston, Dorothy Malone, Anthony Perkins, Sterling Hayden and Toshiro Mifune.

The Four Seasons
ANSWERS

A1. *I Know What You Did Last Summer* (1997)

A2. *Summer of Sam* (1999)

A3. *The Lion in Winter* (1968)

A4. *Suddenly, Last Summer* (1959)

A5. *The Roman Spring of Mrs Stone* (1961)

A6. *Summertime;* also known as *Summer Madness* (1955)

A7. *Autumn in New York* (2000)

A8. *Cheyenne Autumn* (1964)

A9. *Autumn Sonata* (1979)

A10. *Winter Kills* (1979)

Can You Keep It Up for a Week?

QUESTIONS

Q1. This 1988 thriller was set in Newcastle, was directed by Mike Figgis and featured Melanie Griffith, Tommy Lee Jones, Sean Bean and Sting. What's the title?

Q2. She co-starred with Steve McQueen in *The Cincinnati Kid* and with Gregory Peck in *I Walk the Line*, and received an Oscar nomination for *Looking for Mr Goodbar*. Who is she?

Q3. Jan-Michael Vincent, Gary Busey and William Katt played surfer friends in this melancholy 1978 film directed by John Milius.

Q4. Early in her film career, this two-time Oscar winner starred in *Sunday in New York* and *Any Wednesday*. Who is she?

Q5. Thomas Jane played a drug dealer whose attempts to go straight are thwarted in this low-budget 1998 thriller featuring Aaron Eckhart, James LeGros and Mickey Rourke. Name the movie.

Q6. Who played the title role in the scintillating 1940 comedy *His Girl Friday*?

Q7. Barbara Harris and Jodie Foster played the body-swapping mother and daughter in a 1976 comedy remade in 2003 with Jamie Lee Curtis and Lindsay Lohan in those roles. What's the title common to both pictures?

Q8. Name the Irish actor who made his film debut in a brief but significant role as a cold-blooded IRA hitman in *The Long Good Friday* (1980).

Q9. John Travolta came to fame when he donned a white suit and showed off his moves on the dance floor in this 1977 movie, which spawned a hugely successful soundtrack album. What's the film?

Q10. Before Paul Greengrass directed *The Bourne Supremacy* and *United 93*, he made this award-winning dramatisation of events in Derry in January 1972. Name the film.

Can You Keep It Up for a Week?
ANSWERS

ANSWERS TO ROUND 36

A1. *Stormy Monday*

A2. *Tuesday Weld*

A3. *Big Wednesday*

A4. *Jane Fonda*

A5. *Thursday*

A6. *Rosalind Russell*

A7. *Freaky Friday*

A8. *Pierce Brosnan*

A9. *Saturday Night Fever*

A10. *Bloody Sunday*

Alphabet City
QUESTIONS

What words do the acronyms designate in the following movie titles?

Q1. *A.I.* (2001)

Q2. *WALL·E* (2008)

Q3. *M*A*S*H** (1970)

Q4. *D.O.A.* (1950, or 1988)

Q5. *S.W.A.T.* (2003)

Q6. *JCVD* (2008)

Q7. *F.I.S.T.* (1978)

Q8. *L.I.E.* (2001)

Q9. *D.A.R.Y.L.* (1985)

Q10. *C.H.U.D.* (1984)

Alphabet City
ANSWERS

ANSWERS TO ROUND 37

A1. Artificial Intelligence

A2. Waste Allocation Load Lifter – Earth Class

A3. Mobile Army Surgical Hospital

A4. Dead on Arrival

A5. Special Weapons and Tactics

A6. Jean-Claude Van Damme

A7. Federation of InterState Truckers

A8. Long Island Expressway

A9. Data Analyzing Robot, Youth Lifeform

A10. Cannibalistic Humanoid Underground Dwellers

Guess Who's Coming to Dinner

QUESTIONS

Q1. In which 1967 movie does Paul Newman's character eat fifty boiled eggs in an hour?

Q2. In which 2004 documentary does the director live on cuisine from McDonald's for a month?

Q3. In which 1983 comedy does an exceptionally obese diner explode after he completes a gargantuan meal with an after-dinner mint?

Q4. In a hallucinatory sequence from this flamboyant 1975 musical, Ann-Margret is showered with the contents of TV commercials, including baked beans and chocolate. Name the musical.

Q5. By munching on doughnuts and crisps, Charlize Theron gained thirty pounds – and an Oscar – when she played serial killer Aileen Wournos in this 2003 drama. What's the title?

Q6. Having lost sixty-three pounds to play the title role in this intense 2004 drama, Christian Bale had several scenes shirtless, to reveal a scarily skeletal physique. What's the title?

Q7. Ethan Hawke and Vincent Spano starred in this factually based film about Uruguayan rugby players stranded in the Andes after a plane crash and living off the flesh of their deceased teammates. What's the title?

Q8. Shown in competition at the 1973 Cannes Film Festival, this French–Italian co-production featured Marcello Mastroianni and Philippe Noiret and observed four middle-aged men who gorge themselves on food until they die. What's the title?

Q9. In this 1925 silent classic, Charles Chaplin plays a man so desperate for food that he boils his boot and eats it. Name the film.

Q10. The menu begins with turtle soup and features quail in puff pastry shell with foie gras and truffle sauce. The meal gave its title to which Oscar-winning movie from 1987?

Guess Who's Coming to Dinner
ANSWERS

ANSWERS TO ROUND 38

A1. *Cool Hand Luke*

A2. *Super Size Me*

A3. *Monty Python's The Meaning of Life*

A4. *Tommy*

A5. *Monster*

A6. *The Machinist*

A7. *Alive*

A8. *La Grande Bouffe* (also known as *Blow Out*)

A9. *The Gold Rush*

A10. *Babette's Feast*

Shut Up and Sing

QUESTIONS

In which movies did each of the following songs feature for the first time? Most were nominated for Oscars, and quite a few won. The film's release date follows in brackets.

Q1. *Supercalifragilisticexpialidocious* (1964)

Q2. *It's Hard Out Here for a Pimp* (2005)

Q3. *Que Será, Sera/Whatever Will Be Will Be* (1956)

Q4. *Hakuna Matata* (1994)

Q5. *Chattanooga Choo Choo* (1941)

Q6. *On the Atchison, Topeka and the Sante Fe* (1946)

Q7. *Zip-A-Dee-Doh-Dah* (1947)

Q8. *Boogie Woogie Bugle Boy of Company B* (1941)

Q9. *I've Got a Gal in Kalamazoo* (1942)

Q10. *Accentuate the Positive* (1944)

Shut Up and Sing
ANSWERS

ANSWERS TO ROUND 39

A1. *Mary Poppins*

A2. *Hustle & Flow*

A3. *The Man Who Knew Too Much*

A4. *The Lion King*

A5. *Sun Valley Serenade*

A6. *The Harvey Girls*

A7. *Song of the South*

A8. *Buck Privates*

A9. *Orchestra Wives*

A10. *Here Come the Waves*

Mixed Nuts
QUESTIONS

Q1. In a career spanning more than sixty films, Dirk Bogarde received two BAFTA awards and a further four nominations, along with two Golden Globe nominations. How many Oscar nominations did he get?

Q2. A Buster Keaton classic from 1927 and an award-winning John Boorman film from 1998 share the same title. What is it?

Q3. In this 1960 classic directed by Federico Fellini, Anita Ekberg cavorts in the Trevi Fountain. Name the movie.

Q4. Andie MacDowell's southern-US accent was considered too strong for her role as a refined Englishwoman in *Greystoke: The Legend of Tarzan, Lord of the Apes* (1984). Name the actress who dubbed her speaking voice.

Q5. He played the corpse at the funeral gathering at the beginning of *The Big Chill* but his face was never seen. Who is he?

Q6. Best known as an actor, he directed one film, *Doctor Faustus* (1967), and stayed off screen as the narrator of *Zulu* (1964). Who is he?

Q7. Who played John Lennon in *The Hours and Times* (1991) – and again in *Backbeat* (1994)?

Q8. He and Robert Redford made their film debut in the same picture, *War Hunt* (1962), and he went on to direct Redford in seven movies. Name him – and, for good measure, the seven films.

Q9. Name the Oscar-winning director who died at the age of fifty-four in March 2008 and made a cameo appearance as a TV interviewer in *Atonement* (2007).

Q10. In which of the eleven James Bond films he scored did composer John Barry make an uncredited cameo appearance as an orchestra conductor?

Mixed Nuts

ANSWERS

ANSWERS TO ROUND 40

A1. Incredibly, Dirk Bogarde was never nominated for an Oscar.

A2. *The General*

A3. *La Dolce Vita*

A4. Glenn Close

A5. Kevin Costner

A6. Richard Burton

A7. Ian Hart

A8. Sydney Pollack, who directed Robert Redford in *This Property is Condemned, Jeremiah Johnson, The Way We Were, Three Days of the Condor, The Electric Horseman, Out of Africa* and *Havana*

A9. Anthony Minghella

A10. *The Living Daylights*

Movie, Movie
QUESTIONS

Q1. Which 2008 romantic comedy introduced its title character as an actress (played by Kristen Bell) who is co-starring with William Baldwin in a fictional US TV series, *Crime Scene: Scene of the Crime*?

Q2. Name the Hollywood satire that featured a fictional prison movie, *Habeas Corpus*, starring Julia Roberts, Bruce Willis and Susan Sarandon.

Q3. In which film-industry satire does the fictional low-budget melodrama *Home for Purim* generate unexpected Oscar buzz?

Q4. What was the last picture shown in *The Last Picture Show* (1971)?

Q5. Name the movie showing at the Bedford Falls Bijou in *It's a Wonderful Life* (1946).

Q6. Arguably the best movie ever made about making a movie, this 1973 film was set during the shooting of a film entitled *Meet Pamela (Je Vous Présente Pamela)*. What's the title of the movie (in either English or French)?

Q7. In *ET: The Extra-Terrestrial* (1982), ET gets tipsy while watching a movie. Which movie?

Q8. In *Control* (2007), which downbeat German movie does Joy Division singer Ian Curtis watch before his death by suicide?

Q9. What is the movie that gives Woody Allen's suicidal character a reason to go on living in *Hannah and Her Sisters* (1986)?

Q10. Which movie was Martin Cahill (aka The General) returning to Xtra-Vision in Ranelagh, Dublin, when he was killed?

Movie, Movie
ANSWERS

ANSWERS TO ROUND 41

A1. *Forgetting Sarah Marshall*

A2. *The Player*

A3. *For Your Consideration*

A4. *Red River*

A5. *The Bells of St Mary's*

A6. *Day for Night/La Nuit Américaine*

A7. *The Quiet Man*

A8. Werner Herzog's *Stroszek*

A9. *Duck Soup*, featuring the Marx Brothers

A10. *A Bronx Tale*, directed by and starring Robert De Niro

The Family Way
QUESTIONS

Q1. Name the Oscar-winning brother of Oscar-winner Shirley MacLaine.

Q2. Oscar-winner Nicolas Cage is a nephew of which Oscar-winning director?

Q3. And who is the Oscar-winning daughter of Cage's uncle?

Q4. And which director is the ex-husband of that Oscar-winning daughter?

Q5. They married in January 1958, after their first film together, *The Long, Hot Summer*, and teamed up for another nine cinema releases, most recently in the title roles of *Mr & Mrs Bridge* (1990). Who are they?

Q6. This US actress has been married to Gabriel Byrne in three movies and to Liam Neeson in two movies (and in a Broadway play). Name her and the five films.

Q7. In a 1998 Disney-comedy remake, Liam Neeson's wife played the role that featured Maureen O'Hara in the 1961 original. Name the actress and the movie.

Q8. In 1991, Liam Neeson's Oscar-winning mother-in-law played a psychiatrist in a mental-institution drama that won an Oscar for this actress, who received some publicity when she became the mother of twins in the summer of 2008. Name the actress and the movie.

Q9. Name the Oscar-winning father of that mother of twins.

Q10. The actors whose names are the answers to the above two questions played father and daughter in which 2001 action extravaganza?

The Family Way

ANSWERS

ANSWERS TO ROUND 42

A1. Warren Beatty

A2. Francis Ford Coppola

A3. Sofia Coppola

A4. Spike Jonze

A5. Joanne Woodward and Paul Newman

A6. Laura Linney played the wife of a Gabriel Byrne character in *A Simple Twist of Fate* (1994), *PS* (2004) and *Jindabyne* (2006). She was the wife of a Liam Neeson character in *Kinsey* (2004) and *The Other Man* (2008) – and on stage in *The Crucible*

A7. Natasha Richardson in *The Parent Trap*

A8. Angelina Jolie in *Girl, Interrupted*

A9. Jon Voight

A10. *Lara Croft: Tomb Raider*

The Oscar
QUESTIONS

Q1. At the Oscar ceremony in February 2008, one winner was cut short before making an acceptance speech and, unusually, was then brought back on stage to deliver it. Who?

Q2. This renowned director, who never won an Academy Award, was given an honorary Oscar in 1968. 'Thank you' was all he said before walking away, and then returning, to add: 'Very much indeed'. Name him.

Q3. Only two actors have the distinction of winning Oscars for their portrayals of the same character in different films. Name the character, the two actors and the two films.

Q4. Only one winner of the Oscar for Best Actor has received the award for a film which he directed. Who, and in what film?

Q5. In the history of the Oscars, only one actor has been nominated in two different acting categories in the same year for the same film. He won in one of them. Name the actor and the film.

Q6. Only one person has the distinction of winning both an Oscar and a Nobel Prize. Who?

Q7. Only one performer has received two posthumous Oscar nominations in the Best Actor category. Name him and the two films.

Q8. Only one performer has won a posthumous Oscar in the Best Actor category. Name him and the film.

The Oscar

QUESTIONS

Q9. Only five actors share the distinction of collecting two Oscar nominations each for their performances as the same character in different films. Name all five, and the roles and films for which they received the nominations.

Q10. Only three times in the history of the Oscars has the entire speaking cast of a movie been nominated for acting honours. Name the three movies and the nominated actors.

The Oscar

ANSWERS

ANSWERS TO ROUND 43

A1. Marketa Irglova, who shared the Oscar for Best Original Song, 'Falling Slowly', with Glen Hansard

A2. Alfred Hitchcock

A3. Vito Corleone, played by Marlon Brando in *The Godfather* (1972) and Robert De Niro in *The Godfather, Part II* (1974)

A4. Laurence Olivier in *Hamlet* (1948)

A5. Irish actor Barry Fitzgerald, nominated as Best Actor (which he didn't win) and Best Supporting Actor (which he won) for *Going My Way* in 1944. The rules were changed afterwards to prevent such dual nominations.

A6. George Bernard Shaw, who received the Best Writing, Screenplay Oscar for *Pygmalion* (1938), adapted from his stage play

A7. James Dean, who died in 1955, was nominated in 1956 for *East of Eden* and in 1957 for *Giant*

A8. Peter Finch for *Network* (1977)

A9. Bing Crosby as Father O'Malley in *Going My Way* (1944) and *The Bells of St Mary's* (1945), Paul Newman as Fast Eddie Felson in *The Hustler* (1961) and *The Color of Money* (1986), Peter O'Toole as Henry II in *Becket* (1964) and *The Lion in Winter* (1968), Al Pacino as Michael Corleone in *The Godfather* (1972) and *The Godfather, Part II* (1974), and Cate Blanchett as Elizabeth I in *Elizabeth* (1998) and *Elizabeth: The Golden Age* (2007)

A10. *Give 'Em Hell, Harry* (1975): James Whitmore in a one-man show; *Sleuth* (1972): Laurence Olivier and Michael Caine; *Who's Afraid of Virginia Woolf?*: Elizabeth Taylor, Richard Burton, George Segal and Sandy Dennis

The Luck of the Irish
QUESTIONS

Q1. She was born in the Dublin village of Ranelagh in 1920. She went on to star with John Wayne in five movies. Who is she?

Q2. Name the Irish actor who won a Golden Globe for his portrayal of the title role in the 2005 US TV mini-series *Elvis*.

Q3. Name the Irish actor who was replaced by Viggo Mortensen as Aragorn in *The Lord of the Rings: The Fellowship of the King*?

Q4. The opening film at the Seattle International Film Festival in May 2008 was, aptly, the factually based drama *Battle in Seattle*. Name its Irish writer-director.

Q5. Bono and The Edge wrote the title song for which James Bond movie?

Q6. Name the busy Irish actor who appeared in four films released in Ireland over the first four months of 2008: *There Will Be Blood*, *Margot at the Wedding*, *Stop-Loss* and *In Bruges*.

Q7. Name the Dublin-born actress who played the heroine, Dr Elsa Schneider, opposite Harrison Ford in *Indiana Jones and the Last Crusade* (1989).

Q8. Name the Irish director whose films have included *Cal*, *A Month in the Country*, *Stars and Bars*, *Circle of Friends* and *Dancing at Lughnasa*.

Q9. Which acclaimed Irish novelist wrote the screenplays for the romantic triangles *Three Into Two Won't Go* (1969), featuring Rod Steiger, Claire Bloom and Judy Geeson, and *Zee and Co.* (1972), starring Elizabeth Taylor, Michael Caine and Susannah York?

Q10. Ireland's first significant film director, he was born in Rathmines, County Dublin, in 1892 and made his mark in 1920s Hollywood with spectacles such as *The Four Horsemen of the Apocalypse*, starring Rudolph Valentino, and *Scaramouche*, with Ramon Novarro. Name the director.

The Luck of the Irish
ANSWERS

ANSWERS TO ROUND 44

A1. Maureen O'Hara

A2. Jonathan Rhys Meyers

A3. Stuart Townsend

A4. Stuart Townsend

A5. *GoldenEye* (1995), performed on the soundtrack by Tina Turner

A6. Ciarán Hinds

A7. Alison Doody

A8. Pat O'Connor

A9. Edna O'Brien

A10. Rex Ingram

Physical Evidence

QUESTIONS

In each of these films, a principal character loses, or is missing, a part of his or her body. In each case, name the actor and the missing body part.

Q1. *The Big Sky* (1952)

Q2. *Lust for Life* (1956)

Q3. *The Vikings* (1958)

Q4. *True Grit* (1969)

Q5. *Se7en* (1995)

Q6. *Speed* (1994)

Q7. *Mary, Queen of Scots* (1971)

Q8. *Bad Day at Black Rock* (1954)

Q9. *Kingpin* (1996)

Q10. *The Last Woman/La Dernière Femme* (1976)

Physical Evidence
ANSWERS

ANSWERS TO ROUND 45

A1. Kirk Douglas, finger

A2. Kirk Douglas, ear

A3. Kirk Douglas, eye

A4. John Wayne, eye

A5. Gwyneth Paltrow, head

A6. Dennis Hopper, head

A7. Vanessa Redgrave, head

A8. Spencer Tracy, arm

A9. Woody Harrelson, hand

A10. Gérard Depardieu, penis

Of Human Bondage

QUESTIONS

Which 007 movies featured the following songs?

Q1. *We've Got All the Time in the World* (performed by Louis Armstrong)

Q2. *Nobody Does It Better* (Carly Simon)

Q3. *All Time High* (Rita Coolidge)

Q4. *The Look of Love* (Dusty Springfield)

Q5. *You Know My Name* (Chris Cornell)

. . . and who performed the title songs in these James Bond pictures?

Q6. *The Living Daylights*

Q7. *Die Another Day*

Q8. *The Man with the Golden Gun*

Q9. *For Your Eyes Only*

Q10. *Licence to Kill*

Of Human Bondage
ANSWERS

ANSWERS TO ROUND 46

A1. *On Her Majesty's Secret Service*

A2. *The Spy Who Loved Me*

A3. *Octopussy*

A4. *Casino Royale* (1967)

A5. *Casino Royale* (2006)

A6. A-ha

A7. Madonna

A8. Lulu

A9. Sheena Easton

A10. Gladys Knight

Once Upon a Time in the West

QUESTIONS

Name the English-language remakes of these foreign-language productions:

Q1. *Funny Games* (Michael Haneke, Austria, 1997)

Q2. *Ringu* (Hideo Nakata, Japan, 1998)

Q3. *Infernal Affairs/Mou Gaan Dou* (Wai-keung Lau and Siu Fai Mak, Hong Kong, 2002)

Q4. *The Seven Samurai/Shichinin No Samurai* (Akira Kurosawa, Japan, 1954)

Q5. *Yojimbo* (Akira Kurosawa, Japan, 1961)

Q6. *Bob le Flambeur* (Jean-Pierre Melville, France, 1956)

Q7. *La Cage aux Folles* (Edouard Molinaro, France, 1978)

Q8. *Abre los Ojos/Open Your Eyes* (Alejandro Amenábar, Spain, 1997)

Q9. *Le Retour de Martin Guerre/The Return of Martin Guerre* (Daniel Vigne, France, 1981)

Q10. *Le Grand Blond avec une Chausseur Noire/The Tall Blond Man With One Black Shoe* (Francis Veber, France, 1972)

Once Upon a Time in the West
ANSWERS

ANSWERS TO ROUND 47

A1. *Funny Games*

A2. *The Ring*

A3. *The Departed*

A4. *The Magnificent Seven*

A5. *A Fistful of Dollars*

A6. *The Good Thief*

A7. *The Birdcage*

A8. *Vanilla Sky*

A9. *Somersby*

A10. *The Man with One Red Shoe*

Another Time, Another Place

QUESTIONS

Q1. Which offbeat 2000 comedy was based on Homer's *The Odyssey?*

Q2. Who played Achilles in *Troy* (2004), based on Homer's *The Iliad?*

Q3. Brian Cox played Agamemnon in *Troy*. Who played him in *Time Bandits* (1982)?

Q4. Who played Julius Caesar in *Carry On Cleo* (1964)?

Q5. Who played Hecuba in the 1971 Euripides adaptation *The Trojan Women?*

Q6. Name the renowned singer who played the title role in Pier Paolo Pasolini's Euripides adaptation *Medea* (1969).

Q7. Who directed the 1969 film based on the Petronius novel *Satyricon*, set in first-century Rome?

Q8. Set among Roman soldiers on an island in 303 *AD* , this 1976 release was the first feature made entirely with dialogue in Latin. Name the film.

Q9. Which 1999 Irish road movie opens with a quotation from Plato's *The Republic?*

Q10. Which popular 1954 musical was inspired by Plutarch's *The Rape of the Sabine Women?*

Another Time, Another Place
ANSWERS

ANSWERS TO ROUND 48

A1. *O Brother, Where Art Thou?*

A2. Brad Pitt

A3. Sean Connery

A4. Kenneth Williams

A5. Katharine Hepburn

A6. Maria Callas

A7. Federico Fellini

A8. *Sebastiane*

A9. *I Went Down*

A10. *Seven Brides for Seven Brothers*

Multiplicity

QUESTIONS

Q1. 'It's just a jump to the left, and then a step to the right'. The line is from a dance instruction in which musical?

Q2. Madonna, Bob Geldof, Glen Hansard and Andrea Corr are among the singers cast by this knighted director in his movies. Who is he?

Q3. Name the Booker Prize-winning author who wrote the screenplay for the Irish romantic comedy *When Brendan Met Trudy* (2000).

Q4. In which movie does Colin Farrell dismiss history as 'a whole load of stuff that already happened'?

Q5. One of these is *not* a movie title: *Carry On Nurse, Carry On Doctor, Carry On Matron, Carry On Dentist, Carry On Again Doctor*. Which one?

Q6. Only one of these Cannes Film Festival entries did *not* win the Palme d'Or: *No Country for Old Men, Pulp Fiction, Taxi Driver, Dancer in the Dark, Fahrenheit 9/11*. Which one?

Q7. In May 2008, *The Class (Entre les Murs)* became the first French film to win the Palme d'Or at Cannes since *Under Satan's Son* won twenty-one years earlier. Before that, there had been another twenty-one-year gap since a French film took the same prize, in 1966. What was that film?

Q8. Which US city provides the principal setting for these five movies: *Hotel* (1967), *The Big Easy* (1987), *Walk on the Wild Side* (1962), *A Streetcar Named Desire* (1951) and *The Cincinnati Kid* (1965)?

Multiplicity

QUESTIONS

Q9. Running ninety-six minutes without any cuts, this 2002 film is the longest single shot in cinema history. Name the film.

Q10. 'Photography is truth, and cinema is truth twenty-four frames a second.' Which Jean-Luc Godard movie featured that much-quoted observation?

Multiplicity
ANSWERS

ANSWERS TO ROUND 49

A1. *The Rocky Horror Picture Show*

A2. Sir Alan Parker

A3. Roddy Doyle

A4. *In Bruges*

A5. *Carry On Dentist*

A6. *No Country for Old Men*

A7. *A Man and a Woman (Un Homme et une Femme)*

A8. New Orleans

A9. *Russian Ark*

A10. *Le Petit Soldat (The Little Soldier)*

The End
QUESTIONS

Some of these closing lines from movies are immortal; some are memorable for all the wrong reasons. In each case, identify the film.

Q1. 'Well, nobody's perfect.'

Q2. 'I'm an average nobody. I get to live the rest of my life like a schnook.'

Q3. 'Don't let's ask for the moon – we have the stars'

Q4. 'For a moment there, I thought we were in trouble.'

Q5. 'Now, where was I?'

Q6. 'There's no place like home.'

Q7. 'Think of me whenever you drink tea.'

Q8. 'It's okay. We have all the time in the world.'

Q9. 'I'll be right here.'

Q10. 'I'm finished.'

The End
ANSWERS

ANSWERS TO ROUND 50

A1. Joe E. Brown, *Some Like it Hot* (1959)

A2. Ray Liotta, *GoodFellas* (1990)

A3. Bette Davis, *Now Voyager* (1942)

A4. Paul Newman, *Butch Cassidy and the Sundance Kid* (1969)

A5. Guy Pearce, *Memento* (2000)

A6. Judy Garland, *The Wizard of Oz* (1939)

A7. Harrison Ford, *Hanover Street* (1979)

A8. *On Her Majesty's Secret Service*

A9. ET, *ET: The Extra-Terrestrial* (1982)

A10. Daniel Day-Lewis, *There Will Be Blood* (2007)

Notes

Notes

Notes

Notes